[Among the Many Disappearing Things]

[Among the Many Disappearing Things]

poems

Meredith Davies Hadaway

GRAYSON BOOKS
West Hartford, Connecticut
graysonbooks.com

For Eloise English Davies (1920-2014)
Among the many things I owe her.

Acknowledgments

Many thanks to the editors, readers and staff of the following journals that originally published these poems, sometimes under different titles or in other versions:

Birmingham Arts Journal: "[I no longer squander grief]"
bluestem: "Deepening"
Cider Press Review: "Across Time"
Courtship of Winds: "Sky Lessons"
Delmarva Review: "In Green Ink," "On a Broad Reach They are
　　Magnificent Craft," "State of the Union," "Dead are Deadly,"
　　"Spider Web in a Sycamore Tree"
Evening Street: "October: The Week in Review," "Vigil"
failbetter: "My Mother Closes the Book"
Frigg: "Ten"
Good Works Review: "Aubade"
Josephine Quarterly: "Fireflies" (under title "To a Widow, Living Alone")
OPEN: Journal of Arts and Letters: "[Among the many disappearing...]"
Perceptions: "Hokusai's Lions," "Remains"
Press Pause Press: "Spin"
Pretty Owl Poetry: "Birdsong, Whale Song"
Midwest Quarterly: "Swans"
MORIA: "When Dreams Go Walking"
Mudlark: "Notes for My Obituary"
Red Wheelbarrow: "Bloom"
The Round: "Robins"
Rust & Moth: "Zenith"
Sonora Review: "River & Stream"
Southern Poetry Review: "Passage"
The Spy: "Still Life," "Synonyms for Faith"
Summerset Review: "[Among the many disappearing things],"
　　"Synonyms for Faith"

Sweet: A Literary Confection: "[Among the many…]" (under title "Lift")
Synkroniciti Magazine: "Fourth of July" and "By Hand"
Tampa Review: "At the Monterey Bay Aquarium"
Thin Air: "What My Hands Say"
Verdad: "Echo"
Waxing & Waning: "For the Banjo Man"
Words & Whispers: "Weather Report"

This volume would not be possible without the support and
encouragement of James Allen Hall and the welcoming writers, teachers
and students at the Rose O'Neill Literary House and Washington
College. Additional support has come over the years from the Maryland
State Arts Council, Virginia Center for Creative Arts, Eastern Shore
Writers Association, F. David Wheelan and James Dissette of *The
Chestertown Spy*, Carla Massoni of MassoniArt, Kent Cultural Alliance,
and The Bookplate.

Thanks to poets and friends who served as readers and cheerleaders
for this book, especially Lynn Melnick, Erin Murphy, Kelly Lenox, Gale
Rasin, and Kevan Hunt.

Thanks to John Lang for being my partner in this and every venture
with a keen eye and a loving heart.

Contents

One

*Sycamores throw down
their limbs—for only so long
will they tolerate a roof.*

Starstruck

We overlook the violence
of stars, prefer to call them

twinkling, would rather reach
for them, see our wish fulfilled.

In fact they are erratic furnaces
and worse, are leaving us behind

by every cosmic measure.
Stranded on a planet we choose

to plunder, fools and dreamers
rushing toward our last

desire because it sparkles
even as it burns.

Weather Report

A courteous morning—fog
blurring the treetops, a soft
leap from dreams to this.

No breeze, no birds—just
the cars on the highway, yawning
and yawning.

Each day an eagle waits
on the same piling for me
to wonder why.

War and wilderness, one
destroys us, even as we kill
the other.

Raindrops left on the window—
a message in braille reads: *This
storm missed you.*

In Green Ink

Neruda wrote in green ink, to his mind the colour of life and hope.
—*The Telegraph*

It's 9:20 a.m. and Rachel Carson Osprey is
feeding her chick. We call her Rachel because
these birds were rare before the ban on DDT.

Now they patrol the river every spring, reclaiming
nests on poles and pilings, on platforms we have
placed for them. Like this one beside my neighbor's dock.

Rachel hatched three chicks but two are
gone, snatched by owls or eagles or maybe starved
by the stronger sibling.

We read that more than half of osprey chicks do not
survive their first year—and that's with two parents.
Rachel's mate has disappeared—

lost, we think, defending the nest. There was commotion
and a strange gathering of buzzards. Then all was quiet,
only Rachel remaining, with her single chick.

She's still there, this morning, when I raise my
bedroom shade, though she's grown thinner.
She has to feed her chick and then herself.

Fishing's harder when there is no mate to
guard the nest. A month to go before the chick
can learn to fly and fish.

An early breeze has brought relief from yesterday's
humidity. Rachel perches on a pole beside
her nest and stretches wings behind her, turning

slowly, like a weather vane. She chirps to let
the chick know she's close by, though her back is turned.
The chick, a tiny silhouette atop the nest, has also

turned to face the wind, small wings spread behind,
chirping, too, in perfect imitation of the larger bird.
Here, says one. *Here*, says the other.

The nest, a tangle of debris cemented by saliva—sticks
and bark from several seasons, straw from nearby farms,
some packing string from stacks of cardboard waiting

for recycling—everything now flutters in the morning air.
From one side I see two lengths of ribbon waving wildly.
I pick up my binoculars to take a closer look.

It's green, the ribbon—brilliant green. In a private
celebration, it spirals through the sky.

Deepening

"There is no progress, only a deepening" —Marianne Boruch

Like the lines that bracketed my mouth, now
folds so deep that one conceals a scar—*a very polite
cancer*, the surgeon said as he tucked the stitches
inside my face.

Once we dreamed perfection, questioned how
each line could alter to appear more like
the smooth beauty we wished to find. Hard
reflections still mirrored possibility.

Now I stare out windows to glimpse the bruise
of time. Shadows, purplish beneath a glint
of sun off trees, the tilting roof, a kingfisher back
on his piling. Memory, grown deep, is tidal—

it bares the rocks and ruts that mired us—then tucks
them all beneath the water's rising blue.

Birdsong, Whale Song

I read somewhere that if you slow down
      birdsong, you'll hear whale song—the same
            patterns repeating in different tempos.

Somewhere a bird is singing my song.
      When I was born in Naples, my older brothers
            turned my name to birdsong: *Mer-a-dee, Mer-a-dee*

to mimic Italians, who had no "th"
      for the final syllable. To mimic a chickadee
            that appeared in their bedtime stories.

Go ahead, bring us
      a girl, they said. We will change
            her name.

When I married, I changed my name. *Where*
      is your birth certificate? the visiting clerk
            from Social Security asked me.

I don't have one, I said, though
      I had a passport. *You could be*
            deported, the official sighed.

A researcher slowed birdsong down to study
      its patterns. Then he sped up whale song. Somewhere
            in the middle, he found overlap.

I remember a film clip we saw in school. The bottom
      of the ocean, draped with starfish who barely
            moved. Then a simulated version in

"starfish time." Now they lived a lifetime in just one
      minute—fish blinking in and out of the frame like stars
         through strands of cloud on a dark night.

It's all the same—birdsong, whale song—in different time
      signatures. Slow down these lines to hear ice creaking
         as it drifts closer to the sun.

"On a Broad Reach They are Magnificent Craft"

Every poem begins as a blink
in the sky, a slight turn of the

earth. It stretches the length of the
sun to where a cardinal perches, chipping

away at the morning. It gathers the leaves,
arranging them in riddles of rust and

gold, rubs each stone in its path.

Now it is midday and centuries lie
behind us, a litter of bones and

promise beneath the slurry of sand as we
stroll to the river.

Every poem is a long walk, the resurrection
of all the meters that brought us here, past

windows ablaze with sun. Every hand that
twirled a brush or twisted a knot to tether

us to something that lives on wind, bellows
in the breath of the water.

Fourth of July

Tonight the osprey is low
    in her nest, wings spread
        to protect three chicks from
           the violent sky.

Her mate circles overhead
    in protest as air horns
        blast and clouds of sulfur
           float across the dark.

What makes us think
    this night is ours to burn?

Fireflies

i.

Without stars, we must
navigate by what's pulsing
here in front of us.

ii.

Throw the doors open—
whatever comes in, you need
the light and the view.

iii.

Even the journey
that takes you from one room to
another moves you.

iv.

A moist wind carries
the last of the storm. Inside,
too, I feel it go.

v.

Yellow flowers spring
from the tangles. I did not
plant them—they flourish.

vi.

My life, scattered as
moonlight through clouds, still bright in
some of its pieces.

vii.

Pinpricks of light in
tonight's dark furnace, small flames
hide in the ashes.

Swans

At the end of his life, my husband carved nothing
but swans. Small pairs to give to newlyweds
because, he said, swans mate for life. A larger
one for a friend who was leaving his job and moving
away—a swan song, he said.
And now I dust the nearly life-size bird he left
behind on my piano—a wooden body that somehow holds
both ruffled water and a rain-soaked winter sky.

There are two swans found in our region. The "mute,"
invasive and aggressive, was released by accident
and multiplied to choke the local ponds. The one
he made for me is native—swans called "whistling"
for the sound the wind makes in their wings when
they rise in one white breath and fly away.

At the Monterey Bay Aquarium

after Marianne Moore

World
in a world
    where fish swirl overhead, mad race of
    mackerel—it's dizzying,
        this place of ocean art where we stand

packed
shoulder-to-
    shoulder. Tentacles beckoning, fringed
    jellies spread across
        your vision like eye floaters, up and

down;
a blink, then
    gone. Some sequence iridescence while
    others pulse transparent.
        Here the deadly wait to receive their

prey
by hand from
    the diver who submerges twice a
    day to please the crowd.
        Children lean into the swirling kelp

for
a better
    look at the leopard sharks, the blunted
    foreheads of dolphin fish,
        bloated bluefin tuna. The big fish

ate
yesterday,
    the guide tells us, so they are full. Here
    come the sardines—giant globe
        of silvery souls that move as one.

From
somewhere just
    beneath our vision they navigate
    the tank like a single
        creature; hungry, careful, a million

eyes
that do not
    see so much as feel the offering
    that shivers the surface—
        then descends, like motes in a shaft of

sun,
a glitter
    of stardust in a turquoise sea—a
    revival. Enough to
        feed a wavering immensity.

Hokusai's Lions

i.

Haiku-the-Cat is
a small flame that can warm up
or burn down your house.

ii.

A ball of lint
with a gnat inside
orbits my kitchen like
a lost planet.

iii.

While I write poems, my cat chases
his tail. He is likely to catch it.

iv.

Write it! Because words in
        air will leave us even faster
                than our racing hearts.

v.

A cat in the window, the same
color as the sky, but for now
the birds are safe.

vi.

Clutter disarrays
      my life—the way
   of madness,
illness,

    beauty, and
      also love.

vii.

My cat is a dust-shaped object
    chasing dust-shaped
       objects from my heart.

viii.

Absence carves its shape
between the
fingers of oak leaves.
Art is in the air.

ix.

For good luck, Hokusai
drew a lion every day until
he died—this poem
is my talisman.

Three Faces of Eve

A screech owl stares at us from the hole
in a birdhouse we nailed to a tree.

I call her Eve, for the three faces
she presents—one inquisitive, one

grumpy, one all-business as she
surveys the local pickings.

The "screech," for now a throaty
trill, ignored by little birds that hop

from branch to branch. When one strays
too near, an efficient shadow ends it

with a tiny squawk. Now the cries
arise, alarms within the treetops.

Eve returns to her box, lethal face
emerging toward us, one eye fixed,

unblinking, tells us we may be puzzled
but she knows exactly who she is.

State of the Union

Two gulls locked beak to beak,
wings rowing the water and battering the air so

fiercely I think they must be dying—trapped
in this unnatural embrace.

Starvation, drowning—no good can come of this.

And then they break
        apart just long enough for me to see

that this is combat.

The larger gull dives again into
the other, this time hammering the back

of his head. No mercy. The other trying now
to break away.

Another half an hour, their beaks
entwined, a parody of swans' iconic nuzzling.

No fish in sight, no obvious source.
Just two huge birds—the size of eagles—stuck

together, thrashing as the river slides beyond them,
the ebbing tide exposing mud.

Spin

i.

Full moon, crying geese.
Unlike me, they know which way
the wind is blowing.

ii.

Not in your lifetime,
we tell ourselves as fires blaze,
waters rise, ice groans.

iii.

Because we all share
one heart, it is always beat-
ing, always breaking.

iv.

Reeling on all fronts
—earth calls it spinning as it
orbits, unaware.

v.

Too late, we learn that
trees are gods. Their soft breath swells
our lungs as they fall.

[Among the many disappearing things]

Dictionaries, especially old ones
that smell of musty shelves.
Mine was once my mother's—

held all the words of her life,
alongside those of everyone
she knew or never met.

Without algorithm, they spread
before her in waves of possibility,
oceans alive with meaning, definitions

fluid, changed with every reading,
nuanced, complicated, sprawling
across her nine decades.

I remember how she taught me,
night after night, in slowly turning
pages, first to read, then to swim.

Even in Dreams

words jostle and shift, shuffle in
      ill-fitting shoes.

A brain is largely
    ornamental. My hand, far more useful—
      contracting, expanding
        like wood, ice, tides,
      music, light—every day

the sky starts small
    then swells as birds fly through it.
      What is the ratio of bird to air, my hand
        to what it waves through?

In Tibet the holiest funeral is in the sky.
    The dead are fed to sacred buzzards,
      a final kindness, nurturing
    birds who, in turn, lend wings to the soul.

One leaf strokes the sky in falling.

One word beside another, a green bottle,
      an old boot, riding a current to the sea.

Two

I dream an osprey eye
looks deeply into mine.
Spring brings sharp talons.

Weathering

An enormous cloud follows me
    all day, beckoning toward sleep,
threatening to rain. Offering hope one
    shaft of sun might pierce it.

My friend calls this "God Light,"
    when beams pour through looking like
the cover of a religious pamphlet.
    Door to door the followers travel,

offering stapled words, the divine photo—
    Lamp Unto My Feet, the title I recall.
But my sky does not open. The cloud
    persists—*damp* unto my feet. Stays

with me through the morning, wrapped
    around my coffee. When I start the car,
the cloud is there, stretched across the windshield.
    The whole day's tasks unfold in its

moist embrace, every errand shrouded.
    Even sundown sinks beneath
this canopy. Glowing through the dark,
    stars lose their way behind it.

    Extinguished or obscured, I cannot say.
But we are all in this together—head, heart, hand,
    and foot, vapor, crystal, dust.

My Body Decides to Let Me Live

I was prepared to die,
had left instructions,

paid my bills, resigned
my particular self

to the anonymity of tumor,
to a labyrinth of metal

and linoleum. But my limbs
know better, refuse to lie down

beside the room's recliner, rise
up insistent on the glow

of the bathroom, warming
to the touch of a night nurse

who says again in foreign
syllables *no cancer*.

Sky Lessons

i.

Traffic and birdsong
layer in the shifting breeze. What
if we belong here?

ii.

Windows streaked with last
night's rain—light, through each droplet,
writes its own story.

iii.

The eagles are back.
Two bright heads bend over a
fish. We can share this.

iv.

When the wind drops and
water is glass—just the
gust in every breath.

v.

There are days when no
birds sing—only a passing
car in a heavy sigh.

vi.

Season of retreat.
Warm days ignite whatever
cold nights extinguish.

vii.

A great fog has hushed
the world. Now I can hear
the roar inside me.

viii.

Could I find a home someplace
other than this life? Only
if I were looking.

Echo

All week, an osprey chick has been complaining.
These are the toughen-up days when parents

bring no fish. A chick must be hungry to learn
to dive for food. Soon mated pairs will start the long

trip south, leaving their young to follow. The strong
quit chirping, feed themselves, then fly away.

But some years, one stays behind, here
by its nest, not catching on.

For days, the pleading echoes in the river's
hollow sky. My neighbor pulls his boat, I turn

my garden under. Another awkward sadness
of the many we deny. Another

small disaster, one more cry.

Aubade

The slit of light around a door.
Door between my bed and cups of coffee.

My hand cups the glow of your warm shoulder.
The warm that folds our bodies into one.

One body, expelled in every breath.
A breath so light, it scarcely skims the silence.

Light that slips around the edges.
Edges, gleaming, razor sharp.

"Dead Are Deadly"

—news.nationalgeographic.com

In the bath, I see one black
ant trundling across

my rug and, though I hesitate—
apologize—I grab a sandal

so the crush will be complete.
It's hard to kill the big ones

who can ball themselves between
the fibers of a carpet and survive

so much. But this one, dead now
lies in the fringe, forgotten

till I look down later and see
another ant lift up the smeared

body and struggle it toward the edge
of the tub, where I suppose an ant

funeral has now been planned.
I sigh, feel some regret, then take

this mourner out with another slap
of the sandal. Soon two more ants

appear, one to lift each curled
body. Why is there no warning

in this litter of corpses? If Darwin
figures in, they should deduce

my bathroom is a danger zone
and look for shelter in a place where
sandals never tread—but no, they come
in ever greater numbers to collect

their dead. *Enough!* I say, sweeping
the bodies into a dustpan to dump

outdoors. Let them call for the fallen
there, where the wind through the

sycamore drops limb after limb—
but I keep moving.

October: The Week in Review

A seal slapped a kayaker in the face with
an octopus.

An occurrence—he said / she said / said
the octogenarians.

A musical interval but also the first eight
lines of a sonnet.

Speaking of music, does anyone really
play the ocarina?

October is *not* the eighth month of the year.

Occasionally, I wonder about these things.

River & Stream

One empties
   and fills; the other
      trickles. Both
         keep me afloat.

         When talk runs
      out with the tide, only
   silence lets
words rise inside me.

Alone, I feel the wave
   of hour/day/year
      that motions us
         together.

         Guests arrive, then
      leave. Between visits,
   I discover my life all
over again.

Some intrusion—
   like an oar in the water—
      will allow
         me to move.

         Where the current runs
      strong, no stroke will cut
   through it, so I float.
Just float.

Still Life

Flakes tumble from a weighted branch to
rejoin the falling snow.

A small boat nods on its lines.

Water, water, water reclaiming
the shore.

No matter the season, the sycamore drops
its leaves.

Trees beyond trees.

Light off the river—anything
reflected—becomes art.

Our bones will be chessmen for the gods
of tomorrow.

When the vanishing point is still
outside the frame.

Dust ever-changing: In darkness,
dirt. In sunlight, diamonds.

Robins

Dozens mob the winterberry,
      disassembling its red mantle

   bite by bite, berry by berry,
until it stands, stripped

        to its twigs and branches,
a skeleton of former glory, silently

   fingering the staggering
few who remain too fat to fly,

    happy little drunks, harbingers
of nothing but a blank

   window, a bare winter,
      my disappearing gaze.

Bloom

i.

Rainwater, hose water—
the same source, but only one brings
news from thunderous skies.

ii.

Flowers need rain as we
need flowers. They teach us
to bloom.

iii.

My hydrangeas refuse to be
blue. As my friend's hair is now
allowed to be white.

iv.

All I hear from the silent roof:
No rain, no rain, no rain.

v.

The sun burns brighter,
but the moon grows dim as we
open into sky.

vi.

Rose, a messenger.
Lovely name, past tense of *rise*.
Presently, a scent.

vii.

White irises have raised their heads
in a garden I did not plant. They just
appeared—small, ruffled gods.

viii.

Returned like a cat, agile and
sweet, rain swivels at last down
the windowpane.

ix.

Fragrant even in the dark, my roses
always end with weeping.

Spiderweb in a Sycamore Tree

I only spot the long white wisps because they
        hold a carcass, twisting

in the morning breeze.
        Invisible against my roof's light

molding until a puff of air
        disturbs it and I see it holds

a constellation of small bodies—some
        dead, some still scrambling up

the scrim of silky thread—waving
        gently from a higher limb.

By Hand

Strange writing, accumulated
    strokes, notes, harmonies—I made
them all, but none of them is me.

No word for the color of the river, though
    it would have to start with ultra.
This morning's chroma, a gold I cannot touch.

Trees reach their own conclusions
    in a brightening sky.

The sensation, stepping back
    to see what's on the canvas, or the page
where words write themselves.

When a melody arrives, more plaintive
    than any you would wish to sing,
you recognize the dance of spirit—inside out,

outside in—like breathing, easy, unless
    you think about it.

[Among the many disappearing…]

The dial tone—small presence
humming under the breath—prelude

to cascading frequencies still
capable of song and voice—

before an automated menu shut
us out—back when the dullest

sound could cut through both
daylight—and darkness—constant

or stuttering—and, when silence
called, could answer.

Notes for My Obituary

Follow those private hints,
and never leave the premises.
                    —Rumi

i.

The world looks like one thing and feels
          like something else. Small leaves fluttering
                    beneath lingering clouds.

Traffic's soft surf
          promising nothing more
                    or less than breath.

ii.

A baby boy, born safely and on time in the eye
of the pandemic. "Proof" should be his name.

iii.

I try to raise the shade
          and it threatens to
          jam. I hoist it carefully
and leave it up—
if it's going to be stuck, it better let
me see the river.

iv.

On Zoom each Monday night, I find
it reassuring we still gather. In the buzz
of the hive, even fear is comforting.

v.

My loft window puts me at flight height.
We go on—the birds and I.

A forecast gray and rainy day doesn't
matter. The weather is inside me.

vi.

Holding still. I let the days pass through
       me, waiting to see what remains.

Me and the sky—two shades of the same color.

vii.

I miss my mother. Sometimes she is a sharp
inhalation where air used to be.

viii.

Always waiting for the stars
      to align when
        I could be stoking the fires.

ix.

My screen porch at night.
      Soft heat and fireflies.
          Long pauses between
             cars on the bridge.

x.

My father knew the stars—their names
        and constellations. Now when we have

lost our way, they emerge again. Our calendars, our
        signposts—distance and magnitude.

xi.

I read that the imagination "requires sustained
encounters with uncertainty."

xii.

Sunlight should be God enough.

xiii.

Say at the end she saw the river turn
to gold. The trees stood patiently, as they
always do, calming the breath of the sky.

Vigil

What if she outlives me?
Me—trundling through my

day with its careful "to-do"
list. The old cat strutting from

food bowl to spigot on little
matchstick legs that could

ignite at any moment, pausing
to pee whenever, wherever

she feels the urge. I bow to my
feline queen and rise to turn

the knob of the faucet. *Let our
lives flow on*, I say, adjusting

the stream to a trickle.

Three

Still on my feet but
yes, I feel it now, a stone
in my shoe.

When Dreams Go Walking

they wear no clothes in public places,
fall from heights
                    and lose their teeth.

Dreams call for help from mute
telephones, sit down
                    to take exams

in classes they forgot they had signed
up for. They find back stairs,
                    secret rooms,

and hidden gardens at a house they
used to live in. They go dancing
                    with ex-boyfriends,

recall it all, forgive everything,
                    and let them go.
They can fly, they can fly!

And then they come across your parents,
young, and talking once again.
                    They're leaning

toward each other, head to head
in a network of nerve and synapse,
                    alive as ever, as real
                    as anything in love.

Zenith

A black and white tv was always sputtering
    through those early decades. My father,

twisting knobs to keep the picture
    from its nervous twitch. Images reduced

to grainy shadow when the telescoped
    antenna failed, despite a tinfoil flag.

Households gathered by those modest
    screens, cautioned by all mothers if we

sat too close (we sat too close), we would
    ruin our eyes. We watched all night

until an after-hours signal pierced our blurred
    insomnia. I miss the soft glow sustaining

even after turning off the set, a glimpse,
    through ruined eyes, of the afterlife.

Resurrection

AI could bring back Jesus, aggregating
all his words, his known biography—

[Birth: immaculate; Occupation: prophet;
Hobbies: wine making, long walks

on water]—could recreate him from
whatever DNA is on that shroud.

We could question him and he would
answer in AI-generated voices we'd

modulate to sound just like our own.
There is a danger, though, that this

time he'd say, *F— them, Father.*
They know exactly what they do.

For the Banjo Man

We light fires, play
    music, to send him back

to his home in the stars.
    The song goes on through

the night. We strain, we cry, we
    stumble.

    Everything trembles
between shadow and light.

    Small flames burn all night.
When the ashes cool, we sift

    through what remains for a last
glowing ember.

    The lost song returns to me
in small motifs, clipped

    syllables. The lilt of leaves
in wind, tires churning the pavement,

    someone snoring in the next
room. My heart playing bass.

Ten

I know, because I've counted them—the freckles stretched
across your back, the veins that twist around your forearm
and the fingertips, each tapered into smooth nails
with rising crescents. Your hand, a wave alongside
twists of pillowcase and sheet, a cloud formation made
by bodies always shifting. At your wrist, the watch
you cannot hear but here beside my head, its ticking
mechanism making little gasps. A wrist now whittled,
as are all the bones, by years of lifting stones and firewood.
The dog we both loved as you placed her on a last
blanket. Everything now curled around us, floorboards,
walls and windows, ceiling fan that dangles, stopped.
And blinds that pleat the faintest light. Just ten more
minutes of sleep—ten more minutes—ten more—ten.

What My Hands Say

They tell me I am still my mother's
daughter. Resemblance runs deep

in the topography of veins, the tiny
tremor, protruding knuckles, bare

fingertips and bitten nails. One
palm crinkled like a love letter

that never will lie flat again,
creases still visible, lines

that don't quite
meet say, *You will never...you will*

never... But here, hold this: your
fate, your fact, your curving

destiny, crooked at this juncture
and not long—

clumsy—but sometimes
still capable of song.

Landscape, Elegy

Sitting together in tall grass, we listen
as a slight breeze carries off the cargo

of thought. Beneath us, green
tumbles and dips to a place where the valley

can rest before ascending to hill after hill.
An ongoing undulation—like the world breathing

us in and out, even as we do the same. A mysterious
layering of ochre and violet. Old friends sharing

an exhalation in a field of shadow and light—wide
as sky. Brief as morning. The beauty

of hills puts everything else
beyond our sight.

Synonyms for Faith

All day a lone goose stands on the floating
dock. He nibbles at the water—stretches,

preens—but does not fly. No sign

of the flock that was there the day
before. I worry he's injured or maybe

lost his mate. The tide comes in, raising

the wooden slats that hold him, then
retreats. Ducks crowd by and leave again.

The sun moves down the river, tossing

amber light across the lower layer of clouds.
Still there, now a silhouette against the glowing

sky. There is no lonelier sound than the cry

of just-one-goose—unless you hear another
from further down the river. I can't be sure.

I only know the goose is gone now.

That when I look again, I see a pair
of shadows wing their way along

the river's silver surface.

Eclipse

So fiercely tidal, exposing tumbled rock
and furrow—then the water's rise, a crazy-

quilt of bright—but like the moon that falls
away from us in every orbit, we lose

the long day slowly, a change so slight
we do not feel it—

until each shadow blurs across the next
and we wrap ourselves in night.

Remains

i.

I dream my mother and two cats
are alive again but keep escaping. Windows
open. Windows shut.

ii.

A small boat on the
dark river. Lights from the bridge
sway on the surface.

iii.

We no longer see
many stars—what other fires
have we extinguished?

iv.

Water flows around me—grief
and love, the changing tides.

v.

Wave after wave, years
lap at the shore, stack driftwood,
then wash it away.

vi.

Learning that a friend has died
months afterward, same shock—

but without wondering how
we will go on.

vii.

Every drop of river, rain, and sky, an overflow.

viii.

When you are gone, I will
have to learn to write my
name with my
left hand.

[Among the many…]

I'm losing my edge—the doctor
        says my spine is disappearing

from the inside
        out. I'm not surprised. Lately

I feel less and
        less between my

rib and the kingfisher
        at the end of the dock.

Fierce. Light. Of small
        substance. I'm on my way

to hollow—then flight.

Tall Ships

They glide into our small
waterfront, behemoths

from another era. Rigging lit
in glittering constellations

that dazzle from both sky
and water. Maritime cathedrals,

masts and sails for buttresses,
floating out of time

and place as only beauty can.
Sure, our past is troubled,

and the future is unclear.
But the stars that blink beyond

these wavering pennants—
long-extinguished, across

enormous distances—their light
still reaches us.

Passage

In this gray morning
sleep all the moments—

leaves that race across
the driveway, swells

of small black birds, the sweep
of their flocks. A promise

of rain—and then winter.
The faraway cadence

of cars on the highway. Each
carrying passengers to the next

moment—the one where we
will have to let them go.

[I no longer squander grief]

I no longer squander grief,
but save it for enormities

to come. The vandal death
of a sycamore, a friend's

beloved dog—I stop,
I wince and shake my head,

but then move on because
I need my strength and all

my tears for the day I wake
to find—among the song

of ticking pipes, inquiring
birds, and sighing traffic—

your voice has gone.

My Mother Closes the Book

My mother died twice—the first
was the hardest.

Her eyes abandoned her
to shadow and distortion. Exiled

from her world of books,
she drifted.

We brought her audio replacements,
but she complained they shouted.

She missed the quiet journey
through hushed pages, would

sometimes turn them anyway,
fingers skimming every spread.

Near the end, she heard them
whispering. *What do they tell you?*

I asked her. *Shhh*—she said—
this one's the Epilogue.

Across Time

i.

When names come back, they're rarely
those I reach for. It's the mailman who stopped

for a nip; the bride whose purse was stolen
at her own wedding; the piano teacher whose

powdered cheeks rained down on the keys.
Which of them, I wonder, will remember

my name when it is lost to me?

ii.

Time's scalpel takes us limb

from limb with grim precision.

To cut is to cure, the surgeon says.

Time answers with a sunrise.

iii.

The small round case snaps
open to reveal a mirrored lid.

I marvel at its dusty contents
without once wondering whose

image, from deep within the stippled
surface, looks out.

iv.

The world calls to me, strange
    clanking of the furnace, three
        notes in a minor key.

v.

Great winds blow as the earth
lumbers on in its orbit. Hard

days struggle into harder nights.
But this morning is hushed, breath-

less as the sun reclaims the sky, leaf
by leaf, ripple, and blade. I am here.

And whoever you are, you are too.

vi.

To see the world un-

peopled—a field of snow

carved from a white sky.

All that light, all that light.

vii.

In the end, a rose. Because absence
    blooms and blooms again, fading
        softly as it tips toward the sun.

viii.

One breath holds everything: the dust
of all the roads, these words, your name.
Warm bodies, a rotation. As everything
turns, I turn toward you.

ix.

A promise I hope to keep,
    a letter in transit, one more,
        one more of anything

x.

As days grow short my life
returns to me in broken

shards—some gleaming—the dead
appear in dreams, in lost obituaries,

the living turn up, one by one
each trailing a story they

resume, small shafts of light
that pierce the clouds.

xi.

I grow smaller, I grow large. Less
of me in daylight, more in every shifting
shadow. Wax-and-waning like the moon,
so clear tonight. The tide swells with stars
before it dwindles to mud.

xii.

Startled from sleep by the sound
of my name. It's my own voice calling.

xiii.

Trees line the white sky, thick
fog grips their branches. Leaves stopped

dead in their rustling. Beneath
blighted bark, there is another

story. One without me in it.

Notes

"On a Broad Reach They Are Magnificent Craft" was inspired by the sculpture "Broad Reach" by David Hess, and is dedicated to Alex Castro. The title of the poem comes from an entry on "broad reach" from *The Oxford Essential Dictionary of the U.S. Military*.

"Birdsong, Whale Song" and "Spiderweb in a Sycamore Tree" were written as part of a collaborative creative and healing arts experience called "Extraordinary Journey: Expressing Spirit Through Art and Medicine." I remain hugely grateful to Valentina Morani. Dipl.O.M., L.Ac. for including me in that life-changing journey.

"Notes for My Obituary" includes a quote about imagination from Shaun McNiff's book, *Trust the Process: An Artist's Guide to Letting Go*.

"For the Banjo Man" is for Thomas F. McHugh, in memory.

"Landscape, Elegy" was written for and is dedicated to the memory of Daniel P. Richardson.

About the Author

Meredith Davies Hadaway is the author of five poetry collections, including *Small Craft Warning*, a collaborative volume with artist Marcy Dunn Ramsey. Her previous collection, *At the Narrows*, was winner of the Delmarva Book Prize for creative writing. She is the recipient of a Maryland Individual Artist Award, fellowships from the Virginia Center for Creative Arts and multiple Pushcart nominations. For ten years she served as poetry editor for the *Summerset Review*. In addition to her work as a poet and teacher, she is a Certified Music Practitioner, playing harp at the bedside in hospice and hospital settings. Hadaway holds an MFA in Writing from Vermont College of Fine Arts. She is currently the Sophie Kerr Poet in Residence at Washington College in Chestertown, Maryland.

www.ingramcontent.com/pod-product-compliance
Lightning Source LLC
Chambersburg PA
CBHW060346130626
46553CB00003B/1112